THE CAIPLIE CAVES

Karen Solie was born in Moose Jaw, Saskatchewan. She is the author of four collections of poems including *Pigeon*, which won the Griffin Poetry Prize, the Pat Lowther Award, and the Trillium Award for Poetry. She was International Writer-in-Residence at the University of St Andrews in 2011, and is an Associate Director for the Banff Centre's Writing Studio programme. Her poems have been published in the US, the UK, Australia, and Europe, and have been translated into French, German, Korean, Hebrew, and Dutch. Her first UK collection, *The Living Option: Selected Poems*, was published in 2013. She lives in Toronto.

ALSO BY THE AUTHOR

The Road In Is Not the Same Road Out
The Living Option: Selected Poems
Pigeon
Modern and Normal
Short Haul Engine

THE CAIPLIE CAVES

KAREN SOLIE

PICADOR

First published 2019 by House of Anansi
128 Sterling Road, Lower Level Toronto, ON

First published in the UK 2019 by Picador
an imprint of Pan Macmillan
20 New Wharf Road, London N1 9RR
Associated companies throughout the world
www.panmacmillan.com

ISBN 978-1-5290-0532-5

1 3 5 7 9 8 6 4 2

A CIP catalogue record for this book is available from the British Library.

Printed and bound by CPI Group (UK) Ltd, Croydon, CR0 4YY

Visit **www.picador.com** to read more about all our books
and to buy them. You will also find features, author interviews and
news of any author events, and you can sign up for e-newsletters
so that you're always first to hear about our new releases.

CONTENTS

Preface   *xi*

"In this foggy, dispute-ridden landscape"   1

I

The North   5

Sauchope Links Caravan Park   6

Crail Autumn   8

A Plenitude   9

NO 59981 05825; 56.24324° N, 2.64731° W   11

Having abandoned his mission . . .   12

Efforts are made to dissuade him . . .   13

Evidence of his own cult in Pictland . . .   14

"Ethernan" likely derived from the Latin . . .   17

The Desert Fathers   19

"When Solitude Was a Problem, I Had No Solitude"   21

Tentsmuir Forest   23

A Miscalculation   24

The Spies   26

Mercenaries Know There's Always Room for Specialists
  in the Market   28

The Meridian   30

Whose Deaths Were Recorded Officially as Casualties of
  "The Battle of May Island"   31

Song   34

NO 59981 05825; 56.24324° N, 2.64731° W 37

He remembers a friend . . . 38

Like Cormac Ua Liatháin, he sought . . . 41

Hostilities were inevitable among the four peoples . . . 43

Now blood on his lip . . . 45

Tomorrow, for sure, he will make a start . . . 47

A vision . . . 48

He reexamines his practice . . . 49

A visitation . . . 52

He enquires of the silence . . . 54

An Enthusiast 55

From *The Invertebrate Fauna of The Firth of Forth, Part 2, 1881* 57

The Shags, Whose Conservation Status Is "of Least Concern" 60

"Goodbye to Cockenzie Power Station, a Cathedral to Coal" 61

A Trawlerman 64

She Is Buried on the West Braes 66

White Strangers 68

Origin Story 69

Kentigern and the Robin 73

To the Extent a Tradition Can Be Said to Be Developed; It Is More
  Accurate to Say It Can Be Clothed in Different Forms 75

An Unexpected Encounter With He Who Has
  Been Left Alone To His Perils 77

A Retreat 78

Song 79

Song	83
A Lesson	84
The Intercessors	85
Crail Spring	87
The Sharing Economy	88
Time Away with the Error	89
Two Chapters on Ancient Stones	90
Ancient Remedies with Contemporary Applications Currently in Development	92
56.1833° N, 2.5667° W	94
The Isle of May lies just outside the western boundary . . .	95
Its paved road, which has all the appearance . . .	97
Having once dwelt at Caiplie, "place of horses" . . .	99
In a purposeful adoption of an ancient burial site . . .	101
You Can't Go Back	103
Stinging Nettle Appreciation	105
The Hermits	106
Clarity	108
Notes	*113*
Acknowledgements	*117*

For Michael, Linda, Beth, and Stan

ACKNOWLEDGED AS A site of pilgrimage from antiquity, the Caiplie Caves, on the coast of Scotland's East Neuk of Fife, are most consistently associated with the hermit Ethernan. The village and church of Kilrenny, which means "church of Ethernan," are not far away, overlooking the sea. But despite the distribution of Ethernan's name on carved stones and in dedications, where he appears in the accounts he is often sketched only briefly, in passing. Upon returning from study in Ireland, he may have become the first bishop of Rathin in Buchan. Sometimes conflated with Adrian of May, murdered with his fellow monks during a Viking raid on May Island in 875, Ethernan is also supposed to have been the "Itarnan" who "died amongst the Picts" in 669, as entered in the Annals of Ulster. Though some sources imagine him travelling the Great Glen from Iona to Fife in the 640s, or the popular route from Iona east towards Lindisfarne, his link with Iona cannot be confirmed. A number suggest he was an Irish missionary to Scotland who withdrew to the Caves in the mid-7th century in order to decide whether to commit to a hermit's solitude or establish a priory on May Island. This choice, between life as a "contemplative" or as an "active," was not an unusual one to take up among his cohort.

Inconsistencies are not surprising. What is surprising is Ethernan's poverty of supernatural accomplishments. Fantastic tales of early medieval saints, hermits and martyrs in Britain — their feats of strength, endurance, and clairvoyance, their animal associates, meteorological interventions, and divinely assisted acts of revenge — are enthusiastic and plentiful. Ethernan, meanwhile, is said to have survived for a very long time on bread and water.

Ethernan's story still wanders outside the archive, resists a final resting place in the ever-expanding facility of the past. And neither are the Caves the past. As John Berger writes, "The past is not for living in," and the Caves — known locally as the Coves — are very much lived in. Unlike Fillan's Cave in Pittenweem, no interpretive or preservational infrastructure attends them; there is no key to be acquired at a nearby café. Nor is there even a commemorative plaque, such as the one marking Constantine's Cave north on the Coastal Path below the Balcomie Links golf club. People still build fires in the caves at Caiplie, drink, and camp there. Alongside crosses carved over centuries, they record their own symbols and advice, political statements, declarations of uncertainty and love.

It is reason and wisdom which take away cares, not places affording wide views over the sea.

— *Horace, Epistles I, vi, 25–26*

THE CAIPLIE CAVES

in this foggy, dispute-ridden landscape

thus begins my apprenticeship to cowardice

no leeks sprang where I walked

no stags bore beams for my house

neither am I that type of acute person who leads others into battle

or inspires love

all creatures are in exile, says Augustine, but my defeats feel more literal

and fault-based

will my fulfilment be the fulfilment of an error?

an error at the foundation of my life, an error burning in its stove

and this fear to which, as to a bureaucracy

I am repeatedly referred

it is a weak place to meet oneself

grassed roof, dirt for a bed

I don't need to tell you what I thought

I

THE NORTH

Where should we find consolation,
dwelling in the north? Amid the stunted
desperate plant life clinging
to its edges, thriving on atmospheric
vengeance or neglect? Of two moods,
fragile and invasive, it gazes out to sea

as its character bends inland.
And why defend our poignant attempts
at agriculture, the gall
of our entrepreneurs? The defining
mid-winter pageants performed
in a somnolent rage? The leisure class

commends the virtues of hard work
above all else, and we labour under
frost-cramped statutes, the black
letters of legislation, in hog-reek
and land-driven slag, middle-aged
from birth and, given our devotion

to slandering this place, illogically
xenophobic. We could as soon move
south as rise above it. Are sympathies
inseparable from what one does
to stay alive? What is a self
but that which fights the cold?

SAUCHOPE LINKS CARAVAN PARK

Gulls up at dawn with swords and shields,
if dawn only in low season, in the week

we can afford. My love, who negotiated with a Silk Cut
in his wheel hand the unfamiliar roundabout

to the A915 at Kirkcaldy, sweeps droppings
from the paved deck like an owner, with his whole heart.

He grew old not thinking about himself.
So it follows our vacation home is not ours, but let

by the company on certain conditions, for certain uses
pertaining to a quiet enjoyment of sea views

beyond the lower lots, signed-for with the understanding
our initiative shall likewise be applied

at the company's discretion.
The dogs we don't have must be leashed, our wireless

fee charged daily. Here is the rent reminding
tenants they don't own, interest confirming

for the borrower to whom the principal belongs.
Here is the insurance to tell us we're not

safe, and here is the loophole which allows it
to not pay. The week he's scraped together is now his.

My old man, who raises his spirit like a lamp,
collects Stella cans tossed from the raceway

down the hill overwritten with gorse and cow parsley;
and who, discovering the bulb beside the door

burnt out, will, cursing happily, replace it with the spare
I laughed at him for stowing in the glove box.

CRAIL AUTUMN

In a stone village on a stone coast
I tried to convince the storage heaters
to take our relationship to the next level,
spend some of what they'd put away
on me, the rented flat, its walls
three feet thick, stone, and 200 years
older than Canada. What I was
doing there was not to be confused
with doing something. But neither was it
nothing, exactly, and felt necessary,
though hardly a necessity, and so settled
the soot of the subjective over
everything. Objects of my attention
made more of me. The sedimentary shore
broke, like the day, into simple shapes,
which are the most difficult
to explain. In daylight I'd walk, unless
it rained, then hit the Co-op at 4,
before the working people. Suppers were
less simple than negligent, and under
the duvet I'd ruined with ink, the evening's
plan turned to Ativan. Panel shows.

A PLENITUDE

Appearing as though they originate in spiritual rather
than material seed, as proof

we don't know how to properly celebrate
or mourn — bindweed and ox-eye daisy, cranesbill, harebell,

hare's-foot clover, whose ideology is fragrant
and sticky, the underside of reflection blooming

across centuries. Arguments for and against belief
volunteering in equal profusion.

My many regrets have become the great passion of my life.
One may also grow fond of what there isn't

much of. Grass of Parnassus —
and when you finally find it, it's just okay.

But look for lies and you will see them everywhere
like the melancholy thistle, erect spineless herb

of the sunflower family. That the eradication of desire
promotes peace and lengthens life

is time-honoured counsel. Still, you can't simply wait until
you feel like it. The beauty of the campions,

bladder and sea, the tough little sea rocket,
is their effort in spite of, I want to say, everything

though they know nothing of what we mean
when we say *everything*; it is a sentiment referring only

to itself. Purple toadflax, common mouse ear,
orchids, trefoils, buttercup, self-heal,

the *Adoxa moschatellina* it's too late in the year for,
I can hardly stand to look at them.

And all identified after the fact
but for the banks of wild roses, the poppies you loved

parked like an ambulance by the barley field.

Landward, the cave mouth conspicuously dark.
Halfway between Anstruther and Crail,
singular in the vicinity. Prominent
calcareous sandstone outcrop on a raised beach
level, short lengths of passage
and as spectacularly weathered as the coexistence
of good and evil, the earth pigments.

Anchor in five metres, taking care to avoid
the numerous creel markers. At half-tide
a dinghy may be hauled out where the reef buffers
flat rocks, though they are sharp
and landing delicate, if land you must.
Wind may complicate return to the boat. Any visit
is a lesson in how quickly conditions change.

Having abandoned his mission,
Ethernan finds the Fife coast
crowded with solitaries

terrible to see, worse to be anywhere near, these vagrants

in search of a hermitage

men and women, mostly men

in rags overworn with larger rags

no one on whom to practice themselves

poisoned by their personalities, speaking pain

without opening the mouth

like vegetable life, but less reliable, huddled in the light

of the blind upstairs, and those are not the lingering odours of Paradise

yet they do seem free from a townie fear

of unfit, unkind, unmarked places, the undistracted measure

my fellow *peregrini* in self-exile, the form

of ascetic renunciation most available to Irishmen

Efforts are made to dissuade him
from his retreat

dress codes, character disorders

abecedarian hymns of praise

laws

he who does not cut his hair in the Roman manner, must

she who leaves hers uncovered, must not

no consort with pagans, no believing in vampires

no changing your mind, no wandering

can a person be trusted whose principles forbid despair?

I spot the cleric from a distance by his wide sleeves

his minor build's angle of progress

he looks like someone who sleeps for pleasure

that iron bell a tiresome associate, a bit much

and I will soon be in earshot of his sentences

which exude an ugliness arising in nature

as a mix of banality and abundance

Evidence of his own cult in Pictland exists
in the distribution of carved stones
bearing his name

I can't be sure now there ever was humility in it

burning the self as though it were a city

believing the past might be destroyed

and remade

we Companions of God appeared, even to ourselves

to experience our visions as actual contests

confronting dragons as did the Child Jesus

conversing with the irritable waters of the Albus Fons

improving on Servanus' arguments with the devil while striding broad tracts of land

in satisfaction and in duty to the people

to whom we offered evidence of those who lived and died

contrary to nature's precedents

those blessed by the artifacts claimed special talents

certainly, they seemed to get a lot more done

but the veneration of relics became a trade in relics eventually suggesting

our dear saints possessed, in addition to divine attributes

more than the usual number of working parts

to whom belonged all the blood-soaked cloth?

the surfeit of St. Pancras?

corpses piled up until the whole world was a tomb

death lost its autonomy, strange to say, it sickened

the boundary between place and no-place

no longer firm

it reduced our ability to think metaphorically

we believed the things we said because we said them

and as my colleagues grew incapable

of speaking off-brand, in the middle voice

the temper of my own voice drained away

"Ethernan" likely derived
from the Latin "aeternus,"
or "eternal"

until, finally, all was noise

rage and shame of creatures domesticated by brutality

uncanny beings mechanized under the influence

of austerity's single truth

and the amphetamine of perpetual conflict

in a region of caves with a hermit in each like worms in cabbages

a vacancy

deep, vibrant compartments, chimney announced by a draft

that spat on the back of my neck

silence its content, its disposition, and generative

as language is generative

no one word reigns

I was shy, as we are before the original and self-evident

it immediately duplicated itself inside me, more than can be used in a lifetime

my first fire ingling in the recesses, I saw the scars

from its many tenants

THE DESERT FATHERS

With or without a bindle of crystal meth
they made their anchorage in Egypt's
Wadi El Natrun, or the dismantled
Marine Corps training base of Slab City, California,
hard skills in transition, taking losses
and burning, if not with a sensible fire,
in the pride of specialized knowledge.
Snakeman relocates the red diamond rattlesnake
and northern Mojave rattlesnake
from residents' trailers to his own to live
alongside him with the scorpions and guard dogs;
it's tough to have riches and not love them.
St. Anthony sold his land, gave the money to
the poor, yet in his Outer Mountain sanctuary cried
I desire peace, but these bad thoughts
will not leave me. All burned in body,
in contemplation, as the lonely burn,
a musical state. The brethren assemble
for a meal, or, from the last free place in America
watch the Navy at war games bombing
the Chocolate Mountains,
but Snakeman prefers to exercise his hobbies —
salvaging undetonated shells, pointing
guns at people, antagonizing snowbirds
and short-term RVers communally parked
near the East Jesus Sculpture Garden
and preaching the ethics of solitude.
By vocation or necessity the future transforms

in the heat of the impartial desert.
Tourists and scholars of human interest
from villages along the Nile, or funnelled
through Niland, which the census
grudgingly designates "a place," seek insight
but wish someone would do something about the trash.
Leonard Knight's Salvation Mountain beckons
in three-storey robes of multicoloured latex.
He clocked in with a half-bag of cement and some paint
and kept at it for 26 years. But just as Anthony
decamped to his Inner Mountain
so Leonard did to the Eldorado care home,
and even the tattooed hermit of the Isle of Skye
took up a flat in Broadford. A cell
can teach you everything. All it asks is
you give it your mind. Snakeman wars against
the body that would destroy his spirit.
Someday, he says, I will be all flame.

"WHEN SOLITUDE WAS A PROBLEM, I HAD NO SOLITUDE"

Experience teaches, but its lessons
may be useless. I could have done without a few
whose only byproduct is grief;

which, as waste, in its final form,
isn't good for anything.

A helicopter beating all night above the firth,
a druid shouting astrology outside
the off-licence, will eventually
put the Ambien in ambience.

Our culture is best described as heroic.
Courageous in self-promotion, noble
in the circulation of others' disgrace,

its preoccupation with death in a context of immortal glory
truly epic, and the task becomes to keep
the particulars in motion

lest they settle into categories whose opera
is bad infinity.

Isolation. The odd auditory hallucination.

The meagre profile of a widow's cabbagerow
corresponds to needs must,
but also to its architect's state of mind

at the time. Why do I not move on? Why
hang around here while grass
grows up my chimney?

Every choice is a refusal. *For Christ's sake.*
I am guarding the walls. Like punctuation
it could make all the difference.

TENTSMUIR FOREST

The sign denoting a negative quantity indicates,
also, subtraction. The symbol for *equivalence*

means also *alike*. The deadliest mushroom is
among the most delicious. Distinct

in their intensities of purpose. Her children found her

on the kitchen floor, plate on the table,
pan on the stove. A life foraging in these woods,

she should have known. But to pour out
is not to spill. To spill is not to lay oneself down.

A MISCALCULATION

Like a king from a promontory
the kestrel presides from an updraft, an array
of barely perceptible movements sustaining
balance and attention, and the woodmouse,
the shrew, the secondary characters,
know whose watch they're under. There are no

bystanders among them. The razorbill's piety
winters at sea, secular and medium-sized,
black above, white below; while
frontloaded with military tech
gannets send tones of the aquatic scale
straight to the emotional signature clusters,

though we human proprietors of emotion
are to them as circumstantial
as the shadow I cast over a vole's workday,
my presence too general for relevance.
It was November. I made these notes,
then in absentminded self-disgust

set out on the path from Crail
and by sunset, at 4, could neither return
nor make Kingsbarns before dark.
Though no one knew where I was, real danger
lay elsewhere. No cows even. Just sleepless
fields staring skyward and the firth prowling

the forest of itself, what's hidden as well as
what hides it. To turn back would have made sense
but I chose otherwise, a lamp post
at what I assumed was the golf course
a fixed point I couldn't seem to advance on
like a misinterpretation pursued because now

it is your life. Proportion vanished. A creature
scratching at a stone dyke was big as the North
Atlantic, and my body, not as old as when visible
became, not one with mind, but indistinguishable —
consciousness feeling with the blunt toe of its boot
as its footprints fill with groundwater.

THE SPIES

Where two convene, a third is always present.
This makes the world seem small

and satisfies our need
to be observed and understood.

Polishing a cup behind the bar. In the background
weighing grain. Hovering over us

a few paces behind, or racing ahead, innocently
buzzing like a toy, like the boy

who bags your pheasants then
reports you to the king.

The scenery interprets us
and we are also the hyper-vigilant scenery

sanguine in our right to own the frontiers
in our photographs, drop

some payload, linger at neighbours' windows
with trauma sensors all lit up,

to rat each other out
with the assistance of an airborne scrap

of the 21st-century unconscious
beside which the old machines of delivery appear

inefficient, comical, overlarge, like a Quaalude,
quaint as any former bond between

the watcher and the watched.
Laws of causality and continuity reside in

the vertical din. For over such forms as my heart
is wont to range, did my eyes then range . . .

MERCENARIES KNOW THERE'S ALWAYS ROOM FOR SPECIALISTS IN THE MARKET

"Security contractor" is the term preferred
by a growing industry of private actors who,
at the sharp end of operations,

aren't kidding ourselves about the economy.
Money is a country I can take with me.
I walk through the battlefield

as through my home town, self-actuated,
valued for my talents. In this territory
also known as Fuck You. Your home town

is now my home town.
These abstract northern wastes
are even more so when you're in them

fighting alongside those you've fought against.
The Picts, fortunately, are unmistakable
in their fondness for nudity and tattoos,

in their grim, barbaric language
whose struggle to remain alive is bold
and clearly futile. Homer, in Smyrna, blackwater

of the Meles flowing through him,
knew some individuals are born in combat
and others ruined, frantic with belief in meaning

as a thing outside them
they can't find. All saved, nonetheless,
from poverty, dishonour, boredom, irrelevance.

A durable disorder is in our best interest
to sustain, and loyalty to a paycheque purer
than to a man, or god, and more flexible.

Non-linear. Mission-based.
If the plan does not fit the game you see,
call a few audibles, and change it.

THE MERIDIAN

Fishers, who mapped Kilrenny steeple
as a marker to direct them at sea, call it St. Irnie
to this day. I can't bring you back.
My imagination's not enough. Or maybe

it was lost with you offshore among the rigs,
between domestic and foreign sectors, its beacon
unattended. A loved thing shared and doubled
is in solitude never whole again.

The harbour's full of sightsee daycruisers,
private recreational vessels, a few trawlers left
to cross swords for Talisman Energy's odd jobs
on their bellies in the mud. When the sea,

even knowing what it knows, dares flood back in here
with whom will I watch flat fish rummaging
in the sediment, the Canadian sport fisherman
in new gear, baiting his hook with a fillet?

WHOSE DEATHS WERE RECORDED OFFICIALLY AS CASUALTIES OF "THE BATTLE OF MAY ISLAND"

1918, last of January, not late, but dark for hours
Sliding under the Forth Bridge toward the North Sea
Cruisers, battleships, destroyers, and the K-boats

Big, steam-driven pigs
Wallowing in the troughs and undulations
Under radio silence, and no lights
Pursuant to worthless intel
To opinions more plausible in formation than they might otherwise appear
En masse, you can't see past them

    Is he still a boy

Sailing under the flag of error
And, as it happens, low cloud cover
On a collision course with the unforeseen minesweepers

On board K-11, or K-17, turning hard to port
If not exactly on a dime
Or K-14, whose rudder jams full right, K-22 who slams into it
Then is run over by the oncoming HMS *Inflexible*

    Who hears his name called, as if in twilight sleep

A second flotilla, led by HMS *Fearless*
Unaware the ships of the first have turned around

Increases speed to 21 knots
They meet head-on east of May Island, which barely looks up from its desk

Intuition breaks in two and heads for the bottom
Along with the wreck of the K-17
Whose crew is in the water
Feeling the warmth of the self against cold abstraction
No group of people has more in common
More fear in their blood than oxygen at this point

Unstable land, unswimmable water, air needing light
As it was in the chaos at the beginning of creation

Behind *Fearless*, and to avoid HMS *Australia*
K-6 rams K-4, which sinks with all hands
Remaining capital ships and destroyers of the 5th Battle Squadron
Bear down on the scene
On the men in the water
Whose eyesight has never been clearer, how cruel

I saw not it, but the place where it dwells

Chains of the wake around their ankles
Propellers tearing through them
Seven stars of the plough obscured by weather
Badly discordant atoms in the one place night seems to be pouring out of

　　Whose grandfather was a shepherd

How can he sleep in such cold
Face up or face down

In sheets of fuel
The unbreathable aftermath

104 killed, a conservative estimate
No enemy engaged but error
In the historical present, a modest commemorative monument
With its back to the sea

SONG

Ships arrived to harvest souls // I saw stones become a church //
I saw the church filled with gold // and the pit with souls who harvest gold //

I saw more fields cut from the forest // I no longer saw the forest dwellers //
As an egg to a bird, tree to a stone // I saw trees turn into ships, and sail away //

II

Make your preparations. Supplement a lack
of expertise with curiosity undeterred
by the vandalized interior, histoplasmotic
pigeon shit, trash of its pilgrims who've written
on its forehead and eyelids their symbols
of blessing and protection: Pictish z-rod
(indeterminate), crosses Latin and Greek,

Mairi + Ian, Saor Alba. Iron and magnesium,
the contemplative oxides. Axis of
the main cave, NW-SE. You will see,
among spirits of the exhumed, the holdfasts,
will know the place by its local name
and your readiness repaid. Another landmark
fixed in the mind of the navigator.

He remembers a friend
from his travels

dispersed atoms sullenly reconciled, I woke

to a human noise conceived outside me, for once

and a bundle over to which I hauled my body's carbons

a griskin

hard bread

for thirty years an otter brought fish to Paul the Hermit

yes, well

and neither can I subsist on grasses and spring water

as did Kentigern

another story there, his poor mother

what a place

unwilling to let me expire in their quarter

or in the hope it buys favour

people leave food

I wish they wouldn't I wish they would

some remember me from when I was a person

their backs to me now, a child's small frame

or yards of female fabric describing wind direction

Jesus is love, but bank the coals or die

hands wrapped in rags, heaping stones for a cache against

wild pigs and others, light to moderate snow

horizontally north-south

I recognize this rough farm cloth, its provenance

a wife from the hill of daughters

whose husband walked a path as if to shame it

although you did not sit, did not loosen your coatcollar

before first talking to her

I must not soften my blisters with water, she said

and her neighbourhood with druids up to here

The earth may provide for them
but by Christ's fingernails not what grows from or grazes
upon my own. Dogwalkers, granary robbers,
mannequins, litterers,
Brother, their poetry is truly awful.

her warm kitchen, honey and dry leaf smell of cut barley

spade leaning in a corner representing mortality

Eejits drunk and sunburned by the dyke,
one a stretched rope, one a shrivelled root, another
an angry little spider. You laugh,
but when schoolboys pelt them with rocks, God help me, I understand.
To look at them is to have one leap into your hand.

our talk, the good and lowly vegetables she prepared

memory

I would rather starve now than suffer it

Like Cormac Ua Liatháin, he sought
his desert in the ocean

if one asks for a sign

must one accept what's given?

the hazards of catching authority's eye have been well borne out

May Island on the palm of the horizon, take it away

a proper island, unlike Lindisfarne

gifted to beloved Aidan, who is likeable

and good

but one might long even for Iona in sight of this outrage

this wellhead

thorn in the sea

I wanted an answer, not a choice, it's too late in life

a task, if not completed, might at least be finished with

now a cipher has fallen from an ancient book

logos, anti-logos, an intellectual violence

crouched on the offing like a word crossed out

blood

when one doesn't expect blood

see how it draws around itself

the hospital curtain

Hostilities were inevitable among the four peoples
clustered around the Forth-Clyde line

kingdoms like these don't collapse all at once

even in my white martyrdom the wars find me

as far-off fires use the wind, as seeds will

or burrs that travel in the fur

what can I do

a creature isn't thought from its shell, my knife extracts it

to nourish me wasn't in its life plan no kidding

I've settled bottom-first into the mud of this thinking

pulled the mud of it to my chin, but even a toad

leaps through its tent flaps in spring like a one-man band

what can I do, blink first in this standoff with the May

in its cop sunglasses trying to break me

I don't trust it

and who would seek with me a community of refuge there

even among my fellow half-people

denuded of vegetation, all remainder

estranged by wandering from our body mass

if no one follows shall I lie alone

at my own graveside, on a mattress of the dead

with no cover over me

Now blood on his lip
for some reason

Servanus, desiring a place less pleasant, came here

and flourished in an argument

that the authentic sacrifice is a pure mind, clean spirit

conscience without guile

I offer cold, the season working as it should

loneliness, love working as it should

pain, the body working as it should

and failure

a thought indulged in isolation is almost certainly an error

and May the plus-minus sign

final iteration of a declining symbol I sense before opening my eyes in the cave the firth's dogs dug for me

that the wind plays

as it plays us all, without courtesy

exceeding demand somewhat

the last seed heads tearing their hair out

and raw chill I suppose I'm expected to defeat

as a matter of principle

Tomorrow, for sure, he will make a start
on his regimen

the body quickly becomes a burden

puts a strain on the carer

gets wet, gets cold, drags its feet through the 10,000 steps

one wakes at night to the sound of it crying

asking for knowledge they don't make anymore

refusing to go to the spring for water

when in the morning, water is the first thing it wants

he didn't seem right, St. Luke

in the dream, he was not mild

and with my own voice bade me look

where the island, yards from shore

had sent forth a bridge of rock

by which I boarded

it was warm, bright, I was alone

the grey sea growled like a gear

not so much heard as felt

and when I turned back, the cave

had receded to a dot

the May rolled, prepared to dive

He reexamines his practice

maybe it's still too personal, how I'm doing this

moisture in the contemplation oversupplying the contemplated

run-off contributing to the global damp

walls stained with it, rising earth-damp

the May's hair plastered to its skull, mascara running

staring through the rain-streaked window

staring in or staring out

rocks shivering their molecules are coated with the effort

and the spores whose options are always open

who were born ready

engage their locking jaws

then what had no plan is all plan

lichen's vow is to embody the composition of the universe

less meaning than a way for meaning to emerge

rock groans under it, gnashes its teeth

but gives in, as everything does

you wouldn't want to think about it all the time

short, as I am, on deliberate qualities

I would at least rather have death find me breathing normally

even if soaked to the bone in the vanity of seclusion

owing to the excesses of solitude nearly hairless

ascetic to the point of ephemerality and suddenly you can't hold a shovel

for Pelagius, good deeds and actions are born

in the rational mind, not from grace

he didn't believe in original sin

you can imagine the trouble he got into over that

old Pelagius, keeping it dry

the nothing I do, my unmade works, the no one I love

the life brought to naught

but might one's hands not always be empty?

A visitation

Paul, why are you here?

I would sooner send my spirit out walking between the hailstones

than have you drive it to its corner on the fork of your advice

May Island's undead party orchestra is playing behind the wind, the barking seals

and my little fire's jumping like a bird tied to a branch

a mist of souls accumulates above the wave action

there are voices in the particles flung wildly about

but you are not the sea, Paul, you have no reason to be here

you are cold crept in to murder my seedling

your ellipses are the stuff of nightmares

I have outlived my future, why invite its ghosts

to bother me where I sleep?

they laugh at the fool wringing his old hands at having burned the beetle

with the kindling

they laugh because I think I am alive

it confuses me, Paul

do you hear the music inside

the May's everlasting housefire?

do you see the loneliness streaming from its broken windows

like smoke in every direction?

He enquires of the silence

rock ages, is swarmed by a peppery crottle

grasses grow around the crevices small creatures move into

grasses that draw minerals through their stems

I feel it happening all around me

the teachings say no earthly thing is worthy of affection or contemplation

barnacles, mussels, the *Patella vulgata*

look dried out and foolish at low tide

but I see nothing fallen here

when evening in its uniform jangles its key ring

lyrics float through our common hour

if it's of no use to us, is it useless?

if it's useless, does it still not deserve to live?

AN ENTHUSIAST

Endless heritage beneath the heavenly soundshed.
Jet-black amphiboles. Ten varieties of scones
in Elie. Giant centipedes and petrified tree stumps
of the Devonian fossil record. Pyrope garnets at the foot

of Lady's Tower aren't quite rare enough to accrue significant
market value, much like the self-taught experts
in autobrecciation and exfoliation weathering
who work their way to the surface of the Coastal Path

at the close of a hard winter. Amateur geologists,
rockhounds, and collectors may be distinguished
by their commitments to task-specific outerwear
but a bin bag rain poncho is not the measure of a person.

Ideas gather around phenomena as though for warmth.
Between art and science, our method is the stage
upon which the universal plays in the fragment.
Form in number, ratio in form. A nice bit of white-trap

or ironstone in a setting of green tuff
inspires a loyalty appropriate to no other relationship.
In the floodlights of taxonomy subjects evaporate,
at peace, and an uncompromised image steps forward.

I like it at sea level. It's the right amount of exposition for me
on the shores of the Great Archive. When you bring pain,

as you feel you must, when the exhausting singularity
spreads through my limbs, I look to sandstone

comprehending itself by breaking at joints produced
by the forces. To the stacks, preferentially
and justly eroded along their planes of weakness by seas
four metres higher. As again they well may be.

i.

On the long-lines, Newhaven
under the name of *Menipea ternata*

last summer

we dredged several times last summer
on Newhaven pier

we dredged last summer and previously

west of Inchkeith, 5 fathoms

on fishermen's nets, *Cellaria fistidosa*

We've dredged it frequently on the oyster bank
in 14 fathoms off Longniddry

The *Salicornaria farciminoides*
Flustra foliacea

F. carbasea

M. pilosa

C. denticulate, in the firth, not uncommon

very rare
We dredged this species

The *Canda reptans*
of various authors

found it in refuse
Bicellaria ciliata

Bugula avicularia

B. murrayana

is common in the Forth

and took it last summer

of Johnston, and others
in 4 fathoms, at Aberdour

last summer, off Fidra

cast ashore after storms

We dredged it last summer

south-west of Inchkeith, 5 fathoms   9 fathoms

off Aberlady Bay

Vesicularia spinosa   we have dredged in abundance

It's often found deprived of the polypites

The *Serialaria lendigera* tangled in masses   among other Polyzoa or Zoophytes

Awnella fusca   among rejectamenta, on corallines

Styela grossularia   under large stones at Newhaven

Peltogaster paguri   attached to the abdomen
of *Carcinus maenas*   *Lepas anatifera*
to floating timber   *Balanus balanoides*

abundant between tide marks
we have dredged very frequently in pretty deep water

ii.

We have dredged it. We have taken this species.
Dead valves at Cramond Island, and St. Andrews Bay.

T. pullastra, pure white, occasionally.
We dredged it last summer off the Isle of May.

Scrobicularia prismatica sparingly alive at low water.
Empty shells, with valves still united, are commoner.

On the beach. Brought up by storms. *S. piperata*
well preserved, but not living; they lie in a bed of blue clay.

iii.

Limnoria lignorum, we obtained at Elie. *Nephrops*
norvegicus in immense numbers. *Crangon vulgaris*
on Seafield's sandy beaches. *Lithodes maja*, from stomach
of cod. *Porcellana platycheles*, Crail and Fifeness, low
water. *Stenorhynchus rostratus* in near every dredgeful.
Eurynome aspera, Prestonpans and Portseaton.
This deep-water form is rare in the firth. *P. puber*,
caught on deepsea lines, east and west
of Inchkeith, off Fidra, and May. With *M. marmorata*
in roots of *Laminaria,* on the Newhaven shore
after storms. We have dredged it, and also collected it
at Portobello. But *Ophiocomina nigra*, a specimen
from Mr. Damon, marked "Black Rocks, Leith," I have
sought at the lowest spring tides, without success.

THE SHAGS, WHOSE CONSERVATION STATUS IS "OF LEAST CONCERN"

What night-collector conveniently forgot
her bag of demons on the neighbour's roof?
Cackling softly over the stick tool of 4 a.m.,
loosening the drawstring with clothy knee
and elbowings, they'd pop out shaking the dregs
from their hackles, consumed by evil
laughter, ahistorical croaks, benthic creaks,
then shrieks and howling underscored
by homuncular medieval babies in *sotto voce*,
declamations via voice prosthetic, robot
pet sounds, and I lay there cursing them, the whole
family, though I had nothing to be up for.

On vertebral rock near the Caiplie Caves
like shreds of an outline or shadows freed
of their antecedents, they dry their wings,
eyes closed, faces to the sun. Centre of no
universe, they have the run of the great ancillary.
Though likely they loom large in the imagination
of the sand eel whose peripheries
they torment. As their shouting did mine
wee hours in the silt of my own domain before
the chicks fledged, presumably, the parents
moved on. And I missed them then, as we do
the ones loved best when not around.

"GOODBYE TO COCKENZIE POWER STATION, A CATHEDRAL TO COAL"

— *The Guardian, Sept. 15, 2015*

It might've sprouted from the rhizome of the Leven
Syncline, fed on a post-war optimism
without joy, full of use, liberated
from embarrassing sensitivity. Every idea a lesser one
in proximity to its architecture of practice, purity
of self-definition. Cockenzie Station demonstrating
the irreducible — gas, ash, atmosphere
deformed by a temperament

> *(May Island*
> *nostalgic in its visual field, quaint*
> *with legend, relics, conservation, charm,*
> *whose old ways are showing,*
> *infrastructure repurposed,*
> *adapted, added to, full of feeling)*

under which Glenrothes matured.
Sister stations at Kincardine, Methil, Longannet.
Thousands daily down the open pits
three thousand feet into
the Carboniferous East Lothian, obliged
by the Brutalist winding tower. The water used
was town water. Rail-borne, road-borne coal
pulverized, blown to the furnaces

(and Stevenson's lighthouse
a gothic castle, retrofitted
for automation and designated
heritage. May's volcanic columns
are outdated, permanent, proudly
whitewashed in birdshit and myth)

living and dying by viability and the violation
at the core of achievement. Which, at a distance
is restful, has meaning. Two five-hundred-foot towers
visible from Edinburgh
an avant-garde mechanical gesture,
the modern right to accomplish nothing exceptional
and to do it without style. Cultural criticism
at its fullest expression

(martyrdom, murder,
misfortune yielding a surplus of ghosts
for an island one kilometre squared,
if ghosts were an idea still tolerated
by the non-tourism sector; though the non-
tourism sector tolerates what it must)

with the decency to not outlive its service.
Historical preservation averted on closure
once the photographs appeared,
but narrowly: the turbine, condenser,
control panel, fans, and electrostatic precipitators
of mid-century daring, in vintage colours,
fixtures and components exerting
an undeniable sentimental appeal to a heyday

incandescent and wasteful.
It happens to us all. Demolition halted its slide
into the figurative, and the land
newly earmarked for habitat, an eco-village
and cruise ship terminal
on what some are calling the Scottish Riviera.

A TRAWLERMAN

The sea is neither animal
nor god. Won't be tamed or appeased.
Aidan gave his young priest oil
to calm the waves, but myth is most useful
when it rouses a body
to work harder. Body, spirit, fire, and water
having been absorbed into the world
of commerce in which even
seabirds participate. Their convergence
a sign of herring in the Haikes.
Profit unites great distances, yet its heart
beats inside us. But Evelyn,
whatever counts me truly among the living
resides with you. The rest just
perseverance and good gear.

Ran 30 minutes from Fife Ness,
all nets shot by 9, sky looks like wind.
Soon, heavy swell, the underwater cables
writhing. This foul coastline laced in wrecks.
We'll take tea with the black squad
while we can, and your fine bread, Evelyn.
The '38 winter herring overspilled
box and barrel, silvered the piers
at St. Monans, and the market so strong
fish girls' fingernails dissolved
in brine. No one can predict how herring run.
They are a tender species, easily

influenced. It was luck brought them in
with money circulating freely
as the Germans prepared for war.

In the air, wasn't it, like rain, or ash.
A mineral agitation achieved the pitch of an anxiety
that makes things happen.

Once sat women. They sat here, then there.
They got on the odd nerve
and the minister, Cowper, a conflict-driven figure
calm brought out the worst in.
When the boy ran afoul of Beatrix Laing
it started up again.

Pretty Pittenweem, red roof tile
from the low countries. Grey, wind-scoured Pittenweem,
sky preserved in salt.

The church's script rehearsed in the blood
of Patrick Morton, as in us all. In his fits, ague, respiratory distress
it found its actor and its audience.
Maybe his accusations were malicious, maybe not.
The mind casts its own spells.

You don't need telling what we did to Janet Cornfoot.
You know the ingenuity of cruelty's life cycle
as well as I do. Ergot, St. Anthony's Fire
one theory to resolve what is no mystery. Not in America
and not here.

We weren't poisoned,
we were the infected crop passing alkaloids
among ourselves, salivating
the honeydew inoculum and spitting
when we talked, incubating the deformity
that falls to the soil, becomes the soil, the pathogen
our conditions were right for.

Pittenweem, place of the cave, the cell.
Pretty Pittenweem, its wynds to the harbour.

It was as though, once we'd killed her there
lights went up at last orders of a fucked-up session, and we read
on neighbours' faces our own expressions.
Ugly, greedy, wasted.
We'd had plans for Nicolas Lawson
but called time.

Something did not want the best for us, and hid itself
in our confusion. Hidden, it lived
in everything. That we were superstitious, easily led,
afraid of the unfamiliar in familiar ways
could all be true. Still
to those who believe we knew no better
I'd say, we knew.

under the yardlight
the yard an island
walking out of the dark
like wading ashore
    I answered
when they knocked
you have to in this cold
and that Weiser lock
a ten-year-old could force
    their truck died
in the field they said
phones too
where they were hunting
drinking
and couldn't leave the rifles
as no doubt I would agree
I am alone here
    why is that
blizzard a sea
breaking through the windbreak
two men with guns
what could I do
I let them in

ORIGIN STORY

Pregnant by rape, deception,
or in defiance, accounts vary,
Thaney was thrown from the 25th-floor balcony
of Traprain Law by her father, Loth,
a pride-based thinker
consumed by a tyrant's bloody melancholy.

Maybe she loved him.
It doesn't seem possible
but that's never stopped anybody.

As happens in these stories, she survived,
offending the Bass Rock gannets
who thought they'd seen everything

and Loth, who, in his executive hatred
of surprises, set her adrift
in a coracle without oars,
said, Then let the firth's dogs have her.

*

To make our own the righteous anger
that keeps some people alive
feels like doing something

so grief and fear don't stir
under their blanket, don't open their eyes.

So survival does not seem merely accidental
to the indecision when to lay down
the earthly burdens, the way a quality is accidental
to a substance —

        No, not like that,
      she may have thought,
drifting toward the rock that would be named for her,
clutching at its hair, the fish curious
though emotionally disinterested, as fish are.

They crowded these waters for centuries
in case something like this ever happened again.
Until recently. Not many fish now.

*

The extremities numb first,
her body closing the wings of its mansion
to warm a small inner apartment —
a stove, a bulb on a cord.

All night she clung to the hide
of the greenstone, until the tide took her, at dawn
when walls between worlds
are thin as a motel's.

Don't stir, don't open your eyes, not yet.

Thaney, astronaut
of an inhospitable element
like that between units of time
which, overflowing, extinguishes time.

Please can I lay them down.

How long was she out there. An era, floating
in a cortege of unhelpful sea life,

in the imagination of a culture
with a fetish for suffering,
condensed to a bright concentrate
like the picture on an old tube television,

stove inside her, bulb on a cord.
Were she extinguished, it would glow
a little while, not long.

*

Accounts, though varied, say she cried,
prayed, maybe she sang, no one knows
but the double tides at Culross
that brought her ashore. A quirk

of local topography, not the miracle
ascribed to her child, Kentigern,
born on the north beach and discovered by —

with their usual flair

for being at the right place
at the right time —

shepherds, who fetched the monk
Servanus, from whom Kentigern acquired
the pet name Mungo — or, Dear One —
and a leadership role in the militia of Christ.

*

Thaney, burning from her passage
through the semblance

acquired the density of something
about to be lost.

KENTIGERN AND THE ROBIN

A fine day to be cruel. Sunny, with a breeze
to carry their laughter's smoke
across the cloister.

The rot budding at the core of their energies they'd diagnosed
as Servanus' fondness for Kentigern,
who'd washed up on the beach at Culross

like trash in the barrel of his mother
to steal the affection entitled them.
Hatred is a plotting emotion

and gleefully inclusive. Also irksome
the more they discussed it, Servanus' love
for his pet robin, a stupid thing so trusting

it would eat from his hand.
Killing it was a way to toss
their disappointment off an overpass

without dying. To give up, using another's life.
To blame the bastard killed three birds in one.
A person can't just do nothing.

Into the broken little body Kentigern poured a scant ounce of his spirit.
Into the vacuum left behind rolled a pebble from the afterworld.
I thought as much, Servanus said

and summoned the novitiates: See, this boy is above you.
To him, the standard does not apply.
Through this address, the robin sang.

Through prayers, chores, classes, meals,
through late mass and into the night
it sang to young men with their heads in their hands,

to the knowledge of what they'd done with their ability to do so.
Unwound its voice like a rope into the place it had been
where all communication is one-way.

But a part of it wouldn't be called back.
The robin never flew again,
bound as it was to Kentigern by its debt.

TO THE EXTENT A TRADITION CAN BE SAID TO BE DEVELOPED; IT IS MORE ACCURATE TO SAY IT CAN BE CLOTHED IN DIFFERENT FORMS

As three persons in one, I come to this life:
the one in it, the one beside it, the one far away.

As one also are my three enemies, and the effects
of meds taken at mealtimes.

A stable mind wants vigil, prayer, and labour.

A three-legged table fits nicely in its corner
like a soul in the cleanliness of a realm
whose mathematics cannot lead to error.

Spinoza so loved the triangle
he wished to appreciate God that way.

Pythagoras distrusted nature. Its even numbers
were to him, in their easy divisibility, female;

though the four spiritual violences, four heavens, four hells
are, like a six-figure salary,
more than seems, strictly speaking, necessary.

The three ways the devil is among us, you should know them.

And the three waters to which we may be lost
that flow from injury, exhaustion, sorrow.

Five rows of folding chairs were the first thing police saw
in the starved toddler's home, and in the home
the seven symbols, and the five kinds of harm.

In the highest place, without society, of no definite colour, beak in the air
sweetly singing lives the solitary bird.

The three laws of inner recollection —
do not be lukewarm in this work.
Rubbing at your imperfections as at old stains.

The fifteen strengths are outnumbered by what must be learned,
even more so by what must be avoided, a list too long to get into here

but one Socrates may have pondered as for twenty-four hours
he stood motionless in the snow, no harm done
to body or mind,
composed, altered, erotic, detached —

a story told also about St. Columba
who, nicknamed St. Colm by the lowland Scots
was known to the English as St. Qualm, meaning
torment, violent death, destruction, plague.

Cassian's six ranks of angels conform to Columba's,
which Pope Gregory, the Great Administrator, improved upon, adding three.

In Bill Wilson's *Big Book*, twelve steps conquer addiction.
There are twelve rungs on the Desert Fathers' ladder to perfection.

All you have to do to climb the last one is to die.

AN UNEXPECTED ENCOUNTER WITH HE WHO HAS BEEN LEFT ALONE TO HIS PERILS

Coming across a thing like this   it isn't right
          A pile of cast-offs   off-cuts   mistints
          roll-ends   I'm not sure
to whom   but he is an insult   No
          I know you didn't say anything

and anyway   it's no crime to resemble discarded inventory
          not a crime to regard others
with what appears to be only basic species recognition
          his narrowed eyes   and laid-back ears
the unnerving impression he stares at a situation behind us
becoming more and more likely
          You're not one to judge   No

Nor am I of course   but clearly
he does not have both oars in the water   does not try
to spare the soft parts of his footsoles
like the rest of us   When he was a child
did a moth fly into his ear   did he rest too long on a stone
and catch a cold in his head   It's unnatural
          or overly natural   What can one do with someone
from whom nothing can be taken
          He's done it to himself   hasn't he

A RETREAT

My friend A. owns a model of wireless optimism.
Has to recharge sometimes, but otherwise it's always with her.

I'd concluded I don't know how to love without hating.
A. said I needed a break from meaning's narrative, summary aspects,

should spend time with the natural phenomena no speculation can penetrate.
She said to surrender an idea will feel like a new idea.

I took a sleeping bag to a sheltered place, and set out my paraphernalia.
After dark, the sea a television in another room, only the audio reached me.

A sound like traffic. Or wind and rain.
Vague, like the fog in my clothes.

In fact, details of the world at large seemed radically redacted
and a person forced to extrapolate from context.

It's said we must learn to live with our shame, but some people can escape it.
They leave it with someone else, to whom it then belongs.

When I woke, my throat was raw, as if I'd shouted all night, or sung.
Which I might have done, I don't remember, I was so high.

SONG

The cliff face, open and soft // vulnerable, so near the Coastal Path // undermined by the sea and the noise of the sea // backs away slowly, meets no eye //

Waters of the firth like dogs at a fence // and, behind them, May Island // keeping to itself the authoritative word // scans the shore without turning its head //

III

SONG

In the blood month, the dormancies // in its feelings for us, the land cools //
and conversation runs toward the fee // Who once was a friend, we must guard against //

Thing creates thing beyond our compass // They confide in each other, but not in me //
Between silence and language omens proliferate // A queue of seeds in the ground //

A LESSON

The tide rises, a crowd returning from a stadium,
abstract sound of innumerable specifics
reentering the shoreline's boroughs. Wheels clatter
on the rocks of your driveway, headlamps light the wall.
A door opens in the place in you joy leaps to.

There's puttering in the kitchen. Close your eyes.
What might happen this cycle has happened, and a promise kept —
the nightmare rocks and fingery weed-beds banished —

though something more important kicking off elsewhere
already has the water's attention. Yet again it prepares to withdraw
even its neglect. Tidal pools are exposed,
their smell of mortal exchanges.

Nothing exists in darkness that doesn't in the light.
Once, this comforted you.

THE INTERCESSORS

At our disposal are the tools, the DIY project kit.
The project is ourselves. He doesn't talk lack, doesn't
think lack, He thinks like a millionaire, why shouldn't we?
It's our spiritual heritage to secure our prosperity.
The Air1 Team meets daily to forward requests
to the Mighty Warriors Intercessors

Army. Terry from Paisley, who needs help with rent,
whose back pain arouses the neighbours' judgment,
may well be annoyed appeals for prayers
that Tiger the cat be completely cured including cancer
get more traction in the virtual community.
The intensity of my dream made me unclean until evening.

Walking unsteadily on the ice at night outside the beer parlour
we might, like Bothelm of Hexham, fracture an arm;
but whereas by a splinter of Oswald's cross
was he made whole, we may wake more broken, more wrong,
to another in a series of excuses: *My office prevents me
from being with you at this time.* Whenever I take an Aleve,

Terry, I'll think of you. Anonymous thanks us for efforts
compelling her husband — who, though a literary scholar,
is careless with the grammar of eternal salvation —
to sever his link with the other woman,
casting that particular mountain into the sea, etc.
and vouches for the Prayer and Fasting CD, the free relic

with online purchase. One sends a barbarian
to fight a barbarian, in the Roman wisdom.
Spurned by Honorius in a letter suggesting they defend
themselves, in misery the British turned on each other, retreated
to the old hill forts. Trouble, distress, and sorrow ride before
a miracle. After a miracle, well, you know.

There's limited fortune in the world, it seems,
or a distribution problem. But I go to sleep trusting
my damaged face will be restored as a sign
of love. And extend also my intercessions for Helen,
alone since her Westie, old and full of days, "companion
of companions, friend of friends," went the way of his fathers.

CRAIL SPRING

Surprised on returning to find the flat
flooded with light. Merciless,
evaporative, even when overcast, and
as the solstice neared, sanctimonious
in its imperative to productivity.
An expert with his pen light wondering
how you let it get this bad. That tone.
We were out all day in the clarity
of errors multiplied
into reality. Excess weight disclosed
by the indignity of seasonal clothes
and suspicious the promise
of those first fine days wouldn't be
borne out. Children wept with exhaustion
in the playground past 11,
birds prodded awake at 3. So when the haar
sailed in, flags flying, party in a bag,
and took over the streets, we rejoiced
to see our choices diminish along
with the outlines of what they'd wrought.
Otherwise, not a fucking thing.
What could we do but make a weekend of it?

This performance of "I Want My Fucking Money"
broadcast live from the street will conclude
when the last human being on earth
has perished.
    The Freshly Renovated Bachelor Suite
has its ear to the ground, has the ear of the Paying Guest
who's found a bed among the household's automatic functions,
in its grotto of learning experiences (those decor objects from HomeSense's
Blunt Force Trauma Collection), above which the Victorian Charmer charms
in its super-convenient location, and
the Superhosts walk overland.
    A pilot light flickers like an awareness of self.
Chaos whispers through the fittings, patterns in the textiles
repeat, pipes sing, the weeping tile: between sound and silence
is music. In fact, the Paying Guest rises in the middle of the night
to turn off the radio where no radio exists, a storm imminent over the sea,
no, the lake — where we are will come clear in a minute —
    and when the furnace knocks twice
then hesitates
the Paying Guest lying in the lettings
remembers the old joke about the drummer
and now the Paying Guest is laughing on the inside.

TIME AWAY WITH THE ERROR

I need to call it something, if I'm to curse it.
I am known by many names, it intones in its fake voice
as I bail out the drum of the rental flat's unfamiliar
AEG 365 washer/dryer, whose manufacturer is not responsible
for its misuse, for any use contradicting its natural purpose,
but how can one use improperly an appliance
whose purposes are contradictory?
Never has the manufacturer been more remote.
*I am the have-been-made-in and the-potential-for. I am
the wayward wind.* This speaks to the heart of the problem.
One of free will, adds the AEG 365, with
sublime neutrality. I hear the northern waters walk toward me.
Not in my ear, in my wishful thinking.
I hear a message composed across the Atlantic, made possible
by way of the fact that this hour accommodates all hours,
the way of the fact not as straightforward as it seems;
and maybe the message can't find me in my patience,
where the subcrackle of May Island interrupts all signals
from its station in the firth's hard chair, in January's basement light,
big head bent over its transmission, face
scribbled out. *When a bond is broken, energy is released, disperses
and is lost*, offers the electric fire, whose switch
I'm unable to find. No operator's manual for the long night either,
no troubleshooting tips for those of us
who truth can't stop from going
where truth isn't. *But that's what I love about you*, says The Error,
how you really get into it. As if it's the last stupid thing you'll ever do.

TWO CHAPTERS ON ANCIENT STONES

1.

Such is the nervous power of life. Symbols,
allegorical forms, language
signifying less and less
though very slowly.

> Water freezes in the pore fabric of the sandstone.
> There are various physical openings-up.
> Also powdering, topical growth,
> chemical aggression from the carbon of the country

and an all-over blurring of features
in galleries of the fields.

A wedge knocked from the upper face
of the Aberlemno roadside stone released its serpent
back into groundcover of the late 6th century.

2.

Standing stones at Callanish
stare over the head of time, minds
somewhere else.
Arranged in cruciform, an inner circle
from which expanse flows.

In their presence, we are like grasses
at the two-leaf stage, whose eyes
are only beginning to focus,

      faces wet, light rain pattering our jackets,

and where we saw raw land off the A858 is revealed
a framework for acknowledgement.
Precise and generous technology. Alignments stream right
through us.

      Southeast, the Great Bernera Hills,
      the "Old Woman of the Moors."

We don't want to go back to the car.

Speeding ahead in the vehicles of our bodies,
in our clouds of dust,
everywhere we go is in relation to them now.

As if a happiness felt there might shelter, and survive,
even though all that gave rise to it has passed away.

ANCIENT REMEDIES WITH CONTEMPORARY APPLICATIONS CURRENTLY IN DEVELOPMENT

In the company of
heath pea
(or bitter vetch),
suppressor of hunger
and of thirst, or of the need
to attend to hunger
and thirst —
though not of the need
for more bitter vetch
to remain off the lead
of hunger and thirst —
one may go off-road in the clarity
of depletion, the licorice
of depletion, its anise.

And free of the body
on wings of
the inflorescence,
by its standard
and its keel, fairly
glabrous, on freedom's
transethanol,
300 times more potent
than sugar — its bursts
of lateral physical energy
followed by peace
in which to settle the rootstock

among dark tubers,
no pain there —
one might remember
when joy appeared
like a horse
crossing a river.

Joy might appear differently
should it do so again,
bitter vetch
(or heath pea)
prepares it a place
with the broom
of metabolism —
should one be worthy,
having sold the laptop,
purified accounts,
in an emptied room sleeping
on the floor
of the spirit —
fog burned off the senses
and the seconds
on fire.

May Island, born under the firth's unstable bed,
an eruption deep within the ritual subconscious.
Sill of an underworld planed by glaciers
crawling east-northeast. Ragged incursions,
occlusions, perspectival falsehoods
wreck boats. Heavily birded, sealed, befouled
and anointed. Its resting heart rate is very low.

"The Isle of May," imposed upon it
by foreigners from the English Ordnance Survey,
represents it on contemporary maps and charts
though not in the hearts of people with any sense.
Virtue has deserted its brackish wells.
Sanctuary, a grave peril, sunk to its neck.
Small freshwater loch like a light left on.

The Isle of May lies just outside the western boundary
of danger area D607/55

how long have I been sleeping, Paul?

not that anything's changed

the army of black rock marches from the sea

black rock at a military angle and the seabirds, the spies

poor weed at the cave mouth, I thought winter would have killed it

very little sunlight for its use

roots in not much

wound around fingerbones of former occupants maybe

I find their junk lying around

my affection so reckless it tries to animate

cold objects with its friendship

laugh if you will

music at the fold of appearance and disappearance

may be what I'm hearing

played in the octave between two kinds of darkness

the excess of, and absence of, light

from which do you transpire?

creeping through the scurvy grass, going by smell

Paul, I literally see through you

but you don't frighten me anymore, for I have looked into myself

the May is there

idling at the curb in a cloud of exhaust

radio on

its doors all dented

Its paved road, which has all the appearance
of a processional way, must have led
from somewhere, to somewhere

you may think you want to disperse the intermediaries

between your mind and the true mystery

but believe me

you don't

the solitude

there are no two ways about it

you can live here but don't expect it to entertain you

like a can on a fence it will set you up

test on you its experimental drugs

dress you in its homemade clothes

hunger breaking you in two to make you last

things maintain their professional secrecy

and I look down the length of the great indifference as though it were a train

I want to see the end of

it does not end

the silence in this way like noise

as dust and ash are noise

nutrients of meaning and communication used up

one's self is not a well from which to draw endlessly

if you leave the tap open while brushing your teeth

so says the wisdom of the Proverbs

one day you will want that water back

when you find the place you're in

no longer supports life

Having once dwelt at Caiplie, "place of horses,"
known locally as the Coves

yet, with the fuzzy logic of its mobile infirmary

the haar lays a cool cloth upon my brow

May sent into the hall, where it walks up and down

rolling in its mouth the name my parents gave me

visual losses propagate in supersaturated air

what I can't see, I can't see myself in

I don't mind it

some losses bring peace

though others remain audible to the mind's ear

roaring around their tracks on distant raceways

in this radiant simultaneous tense

buoyant mingling of the elements

the nearby newly astonishes

blooms practically sing to the eye

I'm sorry, I can't get over it

groundleaves, grassblades, individuals in groups

communicating through variations in their common forms

I would like to receive the world as equally

tear down the curtains and bring to light the dust

mistaken for emanations of the spirit

In a purposeful adoption of an ancient burial site,
deliberate burning of the ground,
a shroud came to be charred,
and thus preserved

Paul, where have you gone?

only I, it seems, am exactly as I appear

a living argument against this sort of life

but I'm afraid I'm not good

for anything else now

feasting on simple sugars of my indecision

eroding, like the cave

it can't stop thinking

regret for error, forward facing

is fear

both burn

with ambition

and will not abandon me

where are you Paul, the May has struggled to its feet

it's turned its face toward me

it's about to speak

YOU CAN'T GO BACK

The glass factory doesn't control the batch material fed
though its dog door, that it processes according to its design

just as our own apparatus admits raw phenomena, constituents
rough and refined, for consistency some of the broken old stuff, and water

because everything is. Along a sequence of chutes, conveyors, scales,
it proceeds with decibels of the world's nerves jangling.

On Medicine Hat's industrial verge, Dominion Glass released at intervals
balloons of black smoke with fire inside, like ideas

off the top of its head, that like ideas were more impressive
after dark. Never did it not answer the question posed by its existence.

Those nitrogen and sulphur oxides erupting like personality
into the environment heralded the birth of something useful.

Indecision had no business there. Unlike uncertainty, and the so-called
acts of God haunting even the glass factory's most utilitarian

products; unlike second thought's intuitive logic,
which has undoubtedly saved the ass of more than one glass factory

as was the case for United Glass of Edinburgh when Archie Young
crawled through its bowel with a rope around his waist.

When I learned, as a child, the Medicine Hat factory operated
around the clock, lest molten glass harden in its veins, in a heart

whose capacity for heat was limited only by its physical structure —
I feared for it. Hesitation could mean the vital machinery

would be made worthless. As the nuns said of us, good for nothing.
Rough men cried in '67 when United Glass received its closure notice

despite the apparent health of its enterprise, no one could understand it.
Rumours of a clerical mistake that spared a factory in England

at United's expense trickled down from management, but error
had long since crystallized in the system, and it was too late.

STINGING NETTLE APPRECIATION

Would that you had only seen what was not catnip, was not mint!
Sui generis, you crashed its congregation, and now will attend
to your inattention, will heed this understory plant
who knows where its strength lies —

    in histamine, serotonin, acetylcholine delivered
    by the single cells of its stinging hairs. The absence of doubt in its mind
    is felt by you as the burning numbness of an encounter with naturalism
    that advice makes worse.

Soaked or cooked, it soothes the pain it causes. You could just do the work.
A nutritional as well as metaphorical powerhouse,
it kept the northern hermits alive another day
to flog themselves with it.

    Above and belowground parts differ in pharmacological properties.
    Verify your ailment before you approach. Should the previously indicated
    be contraindicated, all the world's vitamins A and C,
    all the protein and iron in the world won't help you.

Where nettle grows, says local custom, so grows the healing dock
whose leaves, broadfaced and not very bright, may initially provide
a cooling sensation, though there's less to affirm its status as a remedy
than there is the merits of a little self-deception.

    Urtica dioica, sting of two houses. To learn this lessens no one's pain.
    The agonies are products, the ancients say. Not voids, or defects.
    Once they exist, they will always exist.
    Comforts can only lie alongside them.

THE HERMITS

Warmth activates the sugars
and sugars rally
in the gorse, in the flowers
it sees with, the scent
that is its voice,
      the non-toxic fragrant wood
good for cutlery, and for burning
though it flares out quickly
unlike smouldering peat. Are they converting

sugars of their loneliness
to conviction? Burning
their sugars on the wicks
of their frailty
one can nearly read by them

      as Fillan read by the light
of his broken arm,
one of the horrible miracles
of the times —
      St. Fillan, the Human Flashlight,
      patron of the mentally ill —

an unenviable between-worlds
position.

      Whereas marsh orchids
fully in this one

change their clothes
out in the open, hard candy
in their mouths, the sugars
plump, round, smooth,
        unlike seawater's jagged molecules
which when drunk like anger
will tear through you.
Like bitterness, desiccate you.

        To survive, suffering burns
the strength of the afflicted. If,
left in Fillan's cave,
bonds of the stricken
were loosened by morning
his spirit had intervened to convert
the molecules of their madness
        and still later did smugglers stash there
some of those little things
that make life worth living.

        The highly edible
sweet gorse flowers
produce a coconut-flavoured wine
if one enjoys the luxury of time
and a tea prescribed in cases
of uncertainty,
        for those who appear
to have lost all hope.

CLARITY

In the centre of the path
near the ruined bothy.

Styrofoam maybe,
a sweater, fishing gear.

As I approached, I saw
it was a gannet, how odd.

How long, then,
before I realized it was dead?

When did my sixth receiver
register the hydrostatic pressure

of fluid newly at rest
between subject and object?

Bill beneath its wing,
the head's saffron

seemed a signal
that should fade, in death.

What killed it
had not been vain

in its signature, allowing
for the vulnerable feet

to be tucked, as is the instinct,
under the quilt of its body.

Cormorants presided
the way they do over the sea's

many funerals. Rock spoke
through its forms

the eulogy: the smaller
is not the lesser stone.

The day's warm air had cold
ribboned through it

like a hotel atrium
built around a stream

or the childhood swimming hole
fed by an artesian current

I visualized as darker
than the surrounding water

and more coherent, its integrity
having not yet degraded.

Much of what I feared then
has happened,

though not always
as I'd feared.

And so much more to fear
than I'd imagined.

On an afternoon beneath
the Quiraing, we watched

the gannets dive,
looked from the cliff edge

straight through the clear water
to the origins of variety.

In addition to the texts noted below, the Preface draws from Peter A. Yeoman's "Pilgrims to St. Ethernan: the archaeology of an early saint of the Picts and Scots," in *Conversion and Christianity in the North Sea World: Proceedings of a Day Conference*, edited by Barbara Crawford (Committee for Dark Age Studies, University of St. Andrews, 1998).

Of valuable assistance for facts and details throughout have been *A Sketch of the History of Fife and Kinross*, by Aeneas James George Mackay (William Blackwood and Sons, 1857); Bede's *A History of the English Church and People*, translated and with an introduction by Lee Sherley-Price and revised by R. E. Latham (Penguin, 1968); and *The Place-Names of Fife*, vol. 3, by Simon Taylor (Oxbow Books, 2009).

Some phrases and details supporting the passages titled with coordinates appear in the Forth Yacht Clubs Association's guide to the Caiplie Caves and the Hermit's Well.

The third couplet of "A Plenitude" owes a debt to Roland Barthes' *The Pleasure of the Text*, translated by Richard Miller (Farrar, Straus and Giroux, 1975).

"*Efforts are made to dissuade him . . .*": Decisions forbidding belief in vampires, growing one's hair, wandering, and changing one's mind following a vow to remain a bride of God, are among the thirty statutes of the First Synod of St. Patrick.

"*Evidence of his own cult in Pictland . . .*": The second line adapts a phrase from Simone Weil's *The Need for Roots*, translated by Arthur Wills (Taylor and Francis, 2001).

"'*Ethernan' likely derived from the Latin . . .*": Lines 10–12 revise phrases from Max Picard's *The World of Silence* (Eighth Day Press, 2002).

"The Desert Fathers" adapts phrases attributed to Abba Moses (b. 330 A.D.) and St. Anthony (b. 251 A.D.). In 2017, an article in the *Independent* christened Slab City "California's most unlikely Airbnb hotspot."

"When Solitude Was a Problem, I Had No Solitude" is a quote from Thomas Merton's *Thoughts in Solitude* (Farrar, Straus and Giroux, 1999). The term "bad infinity" is Hegel's, from *Science of Logic*, edited and translated by George di Giovanni (Cambridge University Press, 2010). The italicized line repunctuates Abba Macarius' response to Palladius, who in retreat complained of making no progress: "Say, for Christ's sake I am guarding the walls." *The Lausiac History of Palladius*, edited and translated by W.K. Lowther Clarke (MacMillan, 1918).

The phrase "tones of the aquatic scale" in "A Miscalculation" is more or less James Frederick Skinner Gordon's, from his 1867 *Scotichronicon*, vol. 1.

The first line of "The Spies" is based on Matthew 18:20. The last inverts a line from St. Augustine's *Confessions*.

The term "durable disorder," which appears in "Mercenaries Know There's Always Room for Specialists in the Market," was coined by the improbably named Sean McFate, senior fellow at the Atlantic Council, professor of War and Strategy at Georgetown University and National Defense University, and a former contractor with DynCorp International.

The *Meridian* was an Anstruther fishing trawler lost in the North Sea east of Aberdeen in October 2006, while on contract as a repair guard vessel for Talisman Energy, a Canadian company.

Italicized line 28 in "Whose Deaths Were Recorded Officially as Casualties of 'the Battle of May Island'" quotes Ovid's *Metamorphosis*, translated by Anthony S. Kline. Line 41 closely follows one of its phrases, and 36 is from Dionysius the Areopagite's *The Divine Names* and *Mystical Theology*, translated by J. Jones (Marquette University Press, 1980). The Royal Navy's hugely expensive K-class submarines, designed in 1913, soon earned the nickname "Kalamity class" for their involvement in serious accidents. Admiral John (Jacky) Fisher, on hearing of their proposed design, responded: "The most fatal error imaginable would be to put steam engines in submarines."

"He remembers a friend from his travels": By the 7th century, druidism had gone largely underground to avoid persecution by Christian clerics. To ensure a continuity of belief, the Catholic church absorbed the stories of pagan deities into those of the saints and appropriated sacred sites for its sacraments.

Line 10 of *"A visitation"* arrived in a text from Ken Babstock.

The "white martyrdom" of *"Hostilities were inevitable among the four peoples . . ."* is one of three categories in the Cambrai Homily, an Irish text from the 7th or 8th century. White martyrdom was used by St. Jerome to describe the sacrifices of the desert hermits — the withdrawal from company, from all one loves, into a strict and often permanent asceticism. A red martyrdom, or blood martyrdom, was violent death resulting from religious persecution. Green (or blue) martyrdom represented self-denial and labour, and while not necessarily a withdrawal from common life, often involved a retreat to the natural world.

The Invertebrate Fauna of the Firth of Forth, Part 2, 1881, was compiled by George Leslie and William A. Herdman, and published from the Proceedings of the Royal Physical Society of Edinburgh, vol. 6.

Lines 7 and 8 of "'Goodbye to Cockenzie Power Station, a Cathedral to Coal,'" revise phrases from Jean Moréas' "The Symbolist Manifesto," published in 1886.

The first line of the second stanza of "She Is Buried on the West Braes" is from the "First Merseburg Charm," a pre-Christian incantation recorded in the 10th century. In the 18th century, at least 26 people accused of witchcraft were tortured and 18 killed in the village of Pittenweem. In March 2012, the village held a referendum on whether to erect Scotland's first official memorial to victims of the trials. The vote being roughly 50/50, the community council decided against support for the memorial, citing fear of damage to the village's reputation.

"White Strangers": By the end of the 8th century, Viking raiders were terrorizing monasteries and communities in Ireland and Britain, and were known by the Irish as *Finngaill* and *Dubgaill* — the Norwegian "white strangers" and the Danish "dark strangers."

The title "To the Extent a Tradition Can Be Said to Be Developed . . ." appears in a footnote to the introduction to *The Theology of Arithmetic*, by Iamblichus, translated by Robin Waterfield (Phanes Press, 1988). The poem draws its numerical assignments from "The Alphabet of Devotion" in *Iona: The Earliest Poetry of a Celtic Monastery* by Gilbert Màrkus and Thomas Owen Clancy (Edinburgh University Press, 1995), and "Dark Night of the Soul," by the 16th-century mystic St. John of the Cross, translated by David Lewis (Thomas Baker, 1908).

The third "Song" uses an idea from Picard's *The World of Silence*.

The Mighty Warriors Intercessors Prayer Army is an online division of Benny Hinn Ministries. The italicized passage revises a fragment from Pope Gregory the Great's letter to the monks he sent to preach to the British in the 6th century. The fifth stanza's final lines draw from *Revelations of Divine Love*, by Julian of Norwich (Penguin, 1999).

Lines referencing Edinburgh's United Glass Ltd. are inspired by the online article "Some recollections by Archie Young Jnr, works' engineer (1962–1967)," edited by Christine Hudson.

The "two kinds of darkness" of "*The Isle of May lies just outside . . .*" are from Dionysius the Areopagite.

Line 19 of "The Hermits" is Dianne Brodie's.

ACKNOWLEDGEMENTS

My sincere thanks to the editors of the publications in which these poems, in earlier versions, appeared:

Times Literary Supplement: "Tentsmuir Forest," "A Lesson," "You Can't Go Back," "Clarity."

New England Review: "A Retreat," "Two Chapters on Ancient Stones," "Stinging Nettle Appreciation."

Ambit: "Whose Deaths Were Recorded Officially as Casualties of 'The Battle of May Island.'"

Poetry London: "Ancient Remedies with Contemporary Applications Currently in Development."

Lemon Hound: "To the Extent a Tradition Can Be Said to Be Developed; It Is More Accurate to Say It Can Be Clothed in Different Forms."

The Forward Book of Poetry 2018: The Best Poems From the Forward Prizes: "An Enthusiast."

POETRY: "The Hermits."

Swimmers: "Origin Story," "Kentigern and the Robin."

Granta: "The Sharing Economy," "A Plenitude," "A Trawlerman."

Wild Court: "He remembers a friend from his travels," "Evidence of his own cult in Pictland exists in the distribution of carved stones bearing his name."

London Review of Books: "An Enthusiast," "Crail Autumn," "Crail Spring," "A Miscalculation."

The Paris Review: "When Solitude Was a Problem, I Had No Solitude."

The Walrus: "The Desert Fathers," "The Shags, Whose Conservation Status Is 'of Least Concern.'"

Harper's Magazine: "The North."

The Scores: "Sauchope Links Caravan Park," "The Spies," "Intercessors," "The North."

Prac Crit: "Mercenaries Know There's Always Room for Specialists in the Market."

Thanks to Carleton Wilson and Junction Books, which published early versions of some of these poems in one of its beautifully designed chapbooks, under the title *Retreats*.

I am grateful to the Canada Council for the Arts, Ontario Arts Council and Chalmers Arts Fellowships, Access Copyright Foundation, Queen's University, Memorial University of Newfoundland, and the Landfall Trust for the time and financial assistance crucial to the completion of this book.

For shelter from the storm, thank you Katherine Ashenburg and Hadley Dyer.

Kitty Lewis, as ever, you have my gratitude and admiration.

Caroline Adderson, Dionne Brand, Greg Hollingshead, Meghan Power, and Shyam Selvadurai, Banff Writing Studio colleagues, your work as writers and as mentors has been an inspiration.

This book has been immeasurably improved by Kevin Connolly, who deftly and subtly picked the locks of doors I didn't know were there. Thanks also to Sarah MacLachlan, Maria Golikova, Janie Yoon, Matt Williams, Alysia Shewchuk, and everyone at House of Anansi Press. Peter Norman, I owe you one. Jonathan Galassi, your support and kind encouragement have supplied fresh oxygen at every stage. Thank you, Don Paterson, for your thoughtful attention, and your ear.

For conversation, advice, wit, and generosity of spirit, thank you Gil Adamson, Ken Babstock, Sheri Benning, John Burnside, Michael Dickman, Michael Helm, Michael Hofmann, Chris Jones, Kimberley Peter, Michael Redhill, Alexandra Rockingham, Declan Ryan, John Sauve, Matthew Tierney, Tara Quinn, Janet Walters, Sheryda Warrener, and Michael Winter.

For my family: everything I write is for you.